SCHOLASTIC

Let's Find Out™

Let's Make Letters

Janice Behrens

Children's Press®
A Division of Scholastic Inc.
New York Toronto London Auckland Sydney
Mexico City New Delhi Hong Kong
Danbury, Connecticut

Literacy Specialist: Francie Alexander, Chief Academic Officer, Scholastic Inc.

Art Director: Joan Michael

Photographs: James Levin (kid letters, buttons, ear, nose, orange slice, train, xylophone); Amy Vangsgard (octopus); ©Alloy Photographer/Veer (ant); ©Bie Bostrom/IPG/SODA (pan); ©Dynamic Graphics, Inc. (umbrella); ©EyeWire, Inc. (fish); ©Frances Clark Westfiled/SODA (book); ©Index Open (car, cat, chair, clock, corn, dinosaur, hamburger, helicopter, ladybug, lamp, marbles, panda, pizza, quilt, ring, saw, seashell, suitcase, teddy bear, wagon, watermelon, wheel, x-ray, zipper); ©IPG/SODA (jump rope, log, pants, soap dish, sock); ©iStock (barn, mitten); ©MorgueFile/SODA (banana); ©Photodisc (apple, bread, cap, dog, duck, elephant, goldfish, guitar, hammer, horse, hose, ice cubes, kite, leaf, lemon, lion, money, orange, ostrich, pear, pepper, pineapple, pumpkin, rose, scissor, spider, stone, tiger, tomato, tricycle, truck, turtle, vacuum, violin, yellow flower, yogurt, zebra); ©Photodisc/SODA (camel, cow, hat, kangaroo, king, mouse, queen, skunk, snake); ©Photodisc/Getty Images (fire, glass, piano, toy bus); ©Photodisc/PictureQuest (milk, shoes); ©Photodisc/Veer (egg, egg carton, goat); ©Sherman Hines/Masterfile (igloo); ©SODA (door, feather, ford, grapes, keys, ladder); iStock/RF (yarn)

Library of Congress Cataloging-in-Publication Data

Behrens, Janice, 1972-
    Let's make letters : ABC kids / written by Janice Behrens.
      p. cm. — (Let's find out)
    ISBN-13: 978-0-531-14867-9 (lib. bdg.)
    ISBN-10: 0-531-14867-X (lib. bdg.)
    1. English language—Alphabet—Juvenile literature. 2. Alphabet
    books—Juvenile literature. I. Title. II. Series.
PE1155.B389 2007
428.1—dc22

                         2006026330

1 2 3 4 5 6 7 8 9 10 R 16 15 14 13 12 11 10 09 08 07

We're the

kids.

Do you think we can make all 26 letters? Watch us try! Here we go!

Aa

All together!
Make an A.

Be smart!
Make a B.

Cc

Come on, kids!
Make a C.

Dd

Do your best!
Make a D.

Which things start with D?

Ee

Everybody!
Make an **E**.

Which things start with E?

Friends can help!
Make an F.

Which things start with F?

Gg

Get ready to go!
Make a G.

Hh

Have some fun!
Make an H.

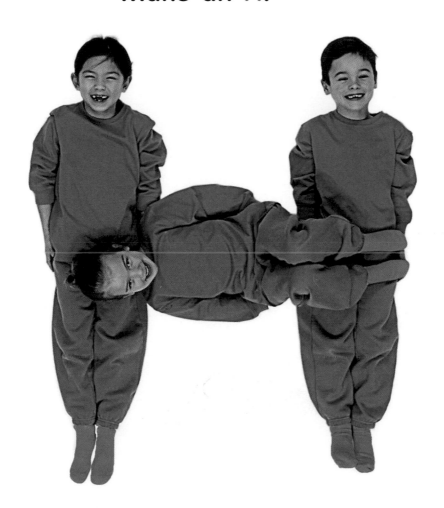

Which things start with H?

I

It's time to try!
Make an I.

Which things start with I?

Jj

Just find a way!
Make a **J**.

Kk

Keep it up!
Make a **K**.

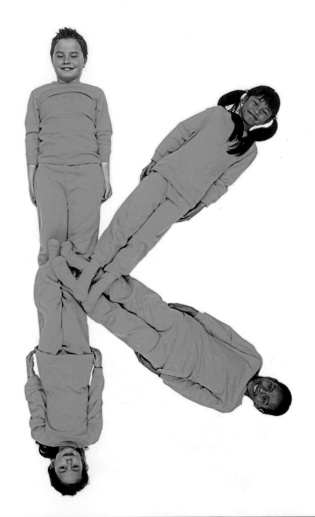

Let's go!
Make an L.

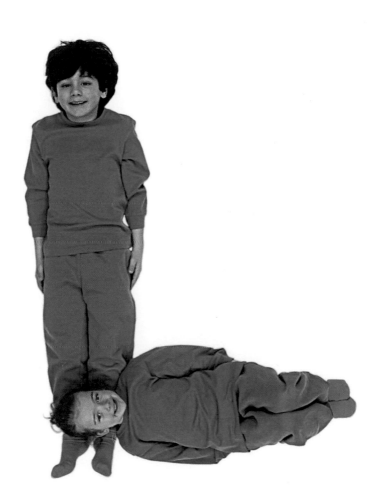

Move together!
Make an M.

Now the next one!
Make an **N**.

On your mark!
Make an O.

Pull together!
Make a P.

Qq

Quick as you can!
Make a **Q**.

Ready to go!
Make an **R**.

Which things start with R?

Slide into place!
Make an S.

Which things start with S?

Tell your friend!
Make a T.

Which things start with T?

Up and under!
Make a **U**.

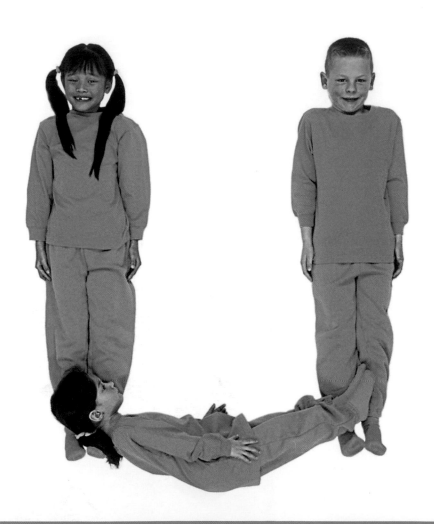

up

Vv

Very good!
Make a V.

Which things start with V?

Ww

What fun!
Make a W.

Which things start with W?

X marks the spot!
Make an X.

You can do it!
Make a Y.

Zoom into place!
Make a Z.

Which things start with Z?

Did you find the things that start with each letter? Here they are!

Ff fire   feather

Gg guitar   goat

Aa apple   ant

Hh hat   hose

Bb book   banana

Ii  igloo   ice

Cc corn   camel

Jj jeans   jumprope

Dd door  dinosaur

Kk king   kite

Ee eggs  elephant

Ll leaf   lion

m	mitten	milk	**Tt**	tomato	tiger
n	nose	nest	**Uu**	up	umbrella
o	ostrich	octopus	**Vv**	violin	vacuum
p	pumpkin	piano	**Ww**	watermelon	wagon
Qq	queen	quilt	**Xx**	x-ray	xylophone
Rr	ring	rose	**Yy**	yarn	yogurt
Ss	sock	scissors	**Zz**	zipper	zebra

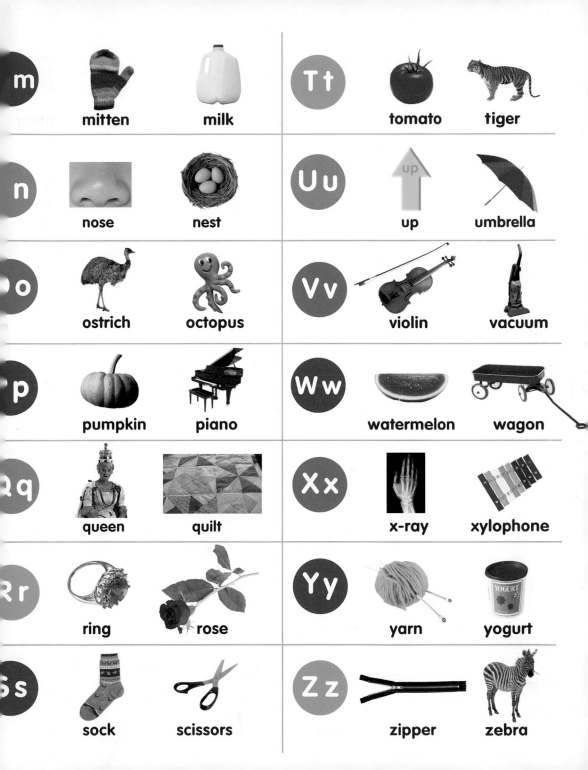

Hooray! We made all the letters!

Can you make letters, too?